Smart Warehousing and Logistics
AI Revolutionizing Supply Chains

Table of Contents

Chapter 1. Introduction

In this Special Report, we delve into the intriguing world of Smart Warehousing and Logistics, a topic that both excites and challenges the modern landscape of supply chain management. At the intersection of technological evolution and operational efficiency, a revolution simmered by Artificial Intelligence (AI) is reshaping the future of the industry. Tackling this somewhat technical subject, we strive to condense complex scenarios into digestible, ground-level insights. We break down the transformations, innovations and potential obstacles autonomous tech may bring to your business infrastructure. Join us as we journey through the gritty details and brighter horizons of smart systems, AI-driven logistics, digital inventory management, and more. This comprehensive exploration is a must-have for industry leaders on the cusp of AI integration, promising to enlighten your perspective and empower your strategic decision-making.

Chapter 2. Introduction to Smart Warehousing and Logistics

Harnessing the power of advanced technology and sophisticated algorithms, the upcoming era of smart warehousing and logistics is set to revolutionize the traditional ways of doing business on multiple fronts. Armed with new tools signified by the integration of artificial intelligence, machine learning, data analytics, automation, and 'Internet of Things', companies are reinventing supply chain processes for increased operational efficiency, consumer satisfaction, and competitiveness.

2.1. The Genesis of Smart Warehousing

To comprehend the potential of smart warehousing, it's imperative first to understand its genesis. Warehousing, at its most fundamental, is the storing of goods prior to their distribution. Traditionally, this was a mostly manual process, fraught with inefficiencies, errors, and waste. At the turn of the 21st century, a technological revolution began to affect most sectors of business, and warehousing was no exception.

Software systems came into use, with the goal of streamlining operations. Warehouse Management Systems (WMS), essentially a suite of software, aimed to manage and control the day-to-day operations in a warehouse. Inventory management, tracking and picking of goods, and executing other warehouse tasks became more efficient with the introduction of these technologies.

However, the true potential of technology dawned when it began to be embedded into physical infrastructure rather than just software. With advent of sensor technology, robotics and other automated processes, the transformation from a traditional warehouse to a smart warehouse was set in motion. Now, the emerging tools of AI, machine learning, data analytics, and IoT, are accelerating this transformation, leading to smarter decisions, superior efficiency, and continuous improvement.

2.2. Realizing the Mechanism of Smart Warehousing

Smart Warehousing aims to introduce technology in each aspect of warehousing operations, to eliminate inefficiencies and enhance overall productivity. There are a few key elements to this:

Automated Guided Vehicles (AGVs): Utilizing physical robots to carry out tasks reduces the dependency on manual labour and consequently removes the associated human errors. AGVs can carry out many tasks within a warehouse, from moving goods to helping in packing, thereby significantly boosting efficiency and speed.

Sensors and IoT: Technology such as Radio Frequency Identification (RFID) allows for real-time tracking of goods. Advanced sensor technology, when combined with IoT, can provide up-to-the-minute inventory levels and ensure accurate and efficient product picking and put-away procedures.

Data Analytics and Machine Learning: One of the most potent tools, analytics helps to make sense of the vast amount of data generated in warehouses. Advanced machine learning algorithms can find patterns, make predictions, and deploy actionable insights to make warehousing more efficient, accurate, and predictable.

2.3. The Transformation to Intelligent Logistics

Just as warehousing is moving from manual to smart, so too is the associated field of logistics. Logistics is the intricate process of managing the movement and storage of goods from origin to consumption. Traditionally, it has been a complex, labor-intensive procedure, involving many steps, many players, and many potential points of failure.

The incorporation of AI has introduced the concept of "intelligent logistics". Such a system can manage and optimize the logistics processes automatically. Such intelligent systems make use of automation, data analytics, machine learning, and IoT to create highly optimized, efficient, and flexible logistics operations.

Operational tasks like route optimization, demand forecasting, freight coordination, and carrier selection can be improved by AI-powered systems, leading to massive savings in both time and money. Moreover, these systems bring transparency and traceability into the logistics processes, thereby enhancing customer satisfaction and trust.

2.4. The Potential Challenges and Obstacles

Despite the bright promises the smart warehousing and logistics holds, the path to their full realization is littered with potential obstacles and challenges.

Data Management: With the infusion of technology comes an abundance of data. Handling this data and making sense of the resulting information overload can be daunting.

Security concerns: As warehouses and logistics systems become more connected, the potential for cyberattacks and data theft increases. Ensuring the security and privacy of information is a significant concern.

Cost and implementation: Transitioning to smart warehousing and logistics requires substantial investments in terms of technology, training, and change management. The associated cost and complexity of the implementation can be major deterrents for many companies.

Adaptability of workforce: With increased automation, the nature of jobs will change. Reskilling workforce into new roles and getting them to adapt to a technologically advanced setup might pose significant challenges.

Despite these challenges, the industry is moving towards a smart future. The narrative is not if, but when and how these smart warehousing and logistics operations will become a standard worldwide. And when they do, the rewards will be considerable—increased efficiency, reduced errors, vast cost savings, and greatly increased customer satisfaction.

And so, at the precipice of a new age, we find ourselves poised for a fascinating journey. The integration of smart systems within warehousing and logistics is not just a trend anymore—it's a necessary progression towards a future shaped by technological innovation and smart operations. With an awareness of what these revolutions offer, and an understanding of the obstacles that lie ahead, businesses can equip themselves better to ride the tide of change and emerge as industry pioneers.

Chapter 3. Understanding the AI Revolution in Supply Chain Management

The profound impact of Artificial Intelligence (AI) on various sectors spells immense possibilities. The sheer intelligence and efficiency of machine-led processes are driving companies to revisit their strategies in supply chain management. This commendable shift from traditional logistical methods to AI-powered operations is what we refer to as the AI revolution.

3.1. Prelude to the AI Revolution

The idea of AI-driven supply chain management is not brand new. The capability to automate certain operations in the supply chain was explored as far back as the 1950s, albeit in a limited and rudimentary way. The rapid advancement of technology over the past few decades, particularly AI, has brought about a tidal wave of transformation that has flooded every aspect of supply chain management.

Today, the term AI revolution refers to the comprehensive integration of AI technologies, like machine learning, deep learning, natural language processing, predictive analysis, and more into the supply chain. This has brought intelligent, self-healing supply chain systems to the fore.

3.2. AI and Supply Chain - A Closer Look

At the heart of any AI-based supply chain management system lies the capability to process a vast quantity of data quickly and accurately. These systems use AI technologies to generate unprecedented insights that help organizations to make informed decisions.

Machine learning algorithms learn from a vast dataset of historical data to predict future trends. As more data fed, these algorithms become more accurate, thereby enhancing their predictive capabilities. This has remarkably improved the accuracy of demand forecasting, stock management, and order fulfillment processes.

Meanwhile, real-time access to data through Internet of Things (IoT) devices has significantly improved inventory management, tracking, and warehousing operations. Thus, AI's impact is not limited to making processes faster and more efficient, but it has also significantly reduced operational and inventory costs while improving customer satisfaction levels.

3.3. Autonomous Tech in Logistics

AI revolution has played a massive part in making autonomous tech a reality in modern logistics. Examples of this include self-driving vehicles and drones. These technologies further reinforce the idea of a highly efficient, human-error free, and sustainable logistical operation.

While the adoption of fully autonomous vehicles is still a few years away from becoming mainstream, companies have started exploring and experimenting with this idea. Drones, on the other hand, have emerged as an excellent logistics tool in remote areas that are otherwise hard to reach by traditional means.

Warehouse operations too have witnessed a radical transformation with the use of autonomously guided robotic systems. These robots can work round the clock, carry heavy loads, and ensure jobs are carried out with pinpoint accuracy, thereby reducing wastage and significantly increasing warehouse capacity and efficiency.

3.4. AI-Driven Inventory Management

One major headache for any logistics service provider or warehousing manager is accurate inventory management. Luckily, AI-powered inventory management systems leverage machine learning and predictive analytics to provide accurate data on inventory levels in real-time.

These systems create a closed-loop, demand-driven supply network that is responsive and adaptive. Such networks can accurately monitor and manage inventory levels using various AI technologies like RFID tagging, drone scanning, and IoT sensors.

By integrating AI and data analytics, companies can now predict demand patterns, optimize stock levels, and make informed decisions about reordering and replenishing the inventory.

3.5. Potential Obstacles to AI Adoption

Despite the benefits, the AI revolution also brings its share of challenges. The most significant challenge is the lack of awareness and understanding of AI technologies among businesses, especially small and medium-sized enterprises. It may also often be limited by budget constraints and a lack of technical expertise.

The idea of AI replacing human labor can also create significant resistance among employees and unions, further complicating the adoption process. There are also ethical and legal considerations related to data privacy and security.

Despite these challenges, the adoption of AI in supply chain management is unstoppable. The key is for businesses to approach it strategically, with a clear focus on understanding how AI technologies can provide real value.

In this era of digital transformation, the AI revolution in supply chain management is not a choice anymore—it's a necessity. Companies that resist this change will find themselves lagging behind as more forward-thinking competitors race ahead. This exhaustive exploration of the AI-driven changes in supply chain management hopes to provide a roadmap to navigate this change and be at the forefront of this exciting revolution.

Chapter 4. The Role of Robotics in Modern Warehouses

Warehousing and distribution centers have traditionally been labor-intensive, with humans painstakingly picking, packing, and moving goods. With the advent of robotics and automation, the warehouse landscape as we know it is undergoing seismic changes.

4.1. Robotics: A Revolution in Warehousing

The use of robotics in warehouses signals a significant shift in the way goods are stored and distributed. Robots, ranging from Automated Guided Vehicles (AGVs) to Autonomous Mobile Robots (AMRs), are increasingly employed to perform tedious or physically demanding tasks, including transporting, sorting, and picking up goods. These robots are designed to navigate warehouse floors independently, recognize objects, and perform tasks with accuracy and speed.

The integration of robotics in warehousing processes often results in increased operational efficiency, reduced labor costs, and improved safety. Robots can work round the clock without breaks, thereby heightening productivity. Furthermore, by taking over repetitive or high-risk tasks, they eliminate the likelihood of employee injuries or fatigue.

4.2. Shift towards Autonomy: How Robots Learn

Robotic systems often employ technologies such as machine learning, computer vision, and sensor fusion to independently navigate through the warehouse environment. Machine learning, a subset of AI, allows robots to learn from their experiences and improve their performance over time. On the other hand, computer vision and sensors enable robots to perceive their environment and interact with it intelligently.

Notably, we see the rise of 'Cobots,' or collaborative robots, which are designed to work alongside humans rather than replace them completely. Equipped with advanced technology, these robots can adapt to the dynamic warehouse environment and complement human skills.

To illustrate one such application, consider the robotic picking systems. Traditionally, manual picking operations have been error-prone and time-consuming. However, with AI-driven robots, commodities can be picked with precision and at rapid speed. For instance, AI enables 'Robo-Pickers' to identify goods of various sizes, shapes, and locations, pick them up in the least damaging way and move them to the required place.

4.3. Potential Obstacles and Resolutions

Despite the exciting prospects, the adoption of robotics in warehouses is not without potential obstacles and pitfalls. First among these is high capital investment. Robotic systems can be expensive to install and maintain. However, over the long term, companies often find that the increase in efficiency and productivity offsets these initial costs. Furthermore, companies can opt for

Robotics as a Service (RaaS) model, wherein they lease robots and pay for their services on a usage basis, reducing the need for high upfront investment.

Another potential obstacle is the technical complexity of integrating robotic systems into existing warehouse operations. It requires careful planning and preparation, including redesigning of warehouse layout and IT system upgrades. Additionally, staff need to be trained to operate and maintain these robotic systems, which may pose a significant challenge.

Nonetheless, with the right planning and execution strategy, these obstacles can be overcome, positioning businesses to gain maximum benefits from robotic integration.

4.4. The Future Ahead: Smart Warehouses

Robotics in warehousing is evolving at a rapid pace. From goods-to-person technologies, where robots bring items to workers, to advancements in perception technology that enable robots to see and interact more accurately with their environment, the possibilities are expanding.

Consider the advent of drones in warehouses. These machines could potentially revolutionize inventory management by soaring up to towering shelves, scanning barcodes, and producing real-time, accurate inventory data.

AI-driven predictive analysis is another promising integration. Algorithms can forecast demand patterns based on sales history, market trends, and festive seasons. Robots can accordingly arrange and rearrange warehouses to ensure fast-moving items are easily accessible, thus streamlining operations.

As we look to the future, the role of robotics in warehousing is set to become even more pronounced. A confluence of AI, machine learning, IoT and Big Data will likely pave the way for fully-automated, 'lights-out' operations, where robots run entire warehouse processes with little to no human intervention.

In conclusion, the adoption of robotics in modern warehouses is proving to be a game-changer. While challenges persist, judicious planning and strategic investments in tech-adoption can empower businesses to overcome these and reap substantial benefits. The smart warehouse, powered by autonomous robots, AI, and data analytics, promises an exciting new era of efficiency and operational excellence.

Chapter 5. Case Studies: How Companies are Implementing AI in Warehouses

The recent past has seen a surge of companies boldly testing the waters of AI integration in their daily warehouse operations. Each example paints a unique picture of the transformative power of technology. Regardless of the industry, size or geographical location, smart warehousing has shown its potential as a value-adding solution.

5.1. Amazon's Robotics Arm

Perhaps the most recognized case is Amazon's adoption of robotics warehousing through its subsidiary, Amazon Robotics. Amazon began its journey into smart warehousing when it acquired robotics company Kiva Systems in 2012. Since then, the mega-retailer has created an automation-driven ecosystem within its humongous fulfillment centers.

Building on Kiva's initial concept, Amazon Robotics develops autonomous mobile robots (AMRs) to move goods around the warehouse. By 2020, the company reportedly had over 200,000 robots working alongside human employees, reducing walking time and increasing efficiency. Furthermore, these robots are guided by AI technologies, including machine learning (ML) and computer vision, which allows them to adapt to changing environments and scenarios within the warehouse.

5.2. Ocado: Grocery Automation

Ocado, the world's largest dedicated online supermarket, has also been heavily investing in AI and robotics for its warehouses. Using a system known as the Ocado Smart Platform (OSP), it automates nearly every aspect of the warehouse operation.

At the heart of the OSP is a hive-grid system where thousands of robots pick and pack customer orders. The system is controlled by an air traffic control technology, ensuring that all robots operate harmoniously within the complex real-time operation.

This approach has revolutionized order accuracy and speed. It has also freed human workers from manual tasks, allowing them to focus on value-added roles such as customer service, troubleshooting, and maintenance.

5.3. Fiege Logistics: AI-Powered Sorting

Fiege Logistics, a globally operating full-service logistics provider, turned to AI and robotics to enhance its sorting capabilities. The company implemented autonomous sorting robots developed by Tompkins Robotics in its operations, with a system known as t-Sort.

The t-Sort system uses theoretically unlimited autonomous mobile robots, which can sort parcels, packets, and other wares to various destinations within the warehouse. These robots use AI and machine learning-based algorithms to optimize their routes and improve efficiency.

The overall result is a marked reduction in manual labor coupled with increased sorting accuracy and efficiency, showing that even specific tasks like sorting can significantly benefit from AI technology.

5.4. Inditex: RFID Technology

At Inditex, the Spanish multinational clothing company best known for its flagship brand, Zara, AI integrates with radio frequency identification (RFID) to optimize inventory management. Inditex has inscribed RFID tags into the security tags of every garment allowing an accurate count of inventory in real-time.

RFID readers placed throughout the distribution centers and stores can pin-point the exact location of each inventory item, improving inventory visibility and enhancing Inditex's ability to restock sold-out items quickly.

The marriage of AI to RFID takes this even further. Machine learning algorithms analyze patterns in inventory movement, predict trends, and suggest restocking schedules. This intelligent inventory management system enables a far more agile response to volatile fashion demands.

5.5. DHL: Predictive Analytics

DHL, one of the world's leading logistics companies, has started using AI to improve operational efficiency. The company leverages predictive analytics to improve forecasting and optimize supply chain processes.

DHL developed a tool called the Global Trade Barometer (GTB) powered by AI, which predicts future trade trends based on large sets of logistics data. The tool enables the company to adjust operations proactively, matching supply with demand more accurately. The GTB also identifies potential supply chain disruptions, allowing DHL to implement contingency measures in a timely manner.

To sum up, these case studies highlight the diverse ways AI can revolutionize warehousing and logistics --- from AMRs and automated picking systems to intelligent inventory management and predictive analytics. As the technology continues to evolve, businesses worldwide are waking up to the possibility of harnessing AI to solve operational inefficiencies. With each successful implementation, they are redefining the industry's best practices and setting the stage for a smart and more efficient future.

Chapter 6. Increased Efficiency: Predictive Analytics in Inventory Management

Inventory management is an integral aspect of any logistics and supply chain operation. Facilitating the smooth flow of goods from the warehouse to the destination, it significantly determines the efficiency of a supply chain. Traditionally, these operations heavily relied on manual inputs and human discretion, but with the rise of artificial intelligence (AI), predictive analytics is now playing a vital role in elevating inventory management to new heights of efficiency. Offering a slew of benefits, such as increased accuracy, cost-efficiency, and scalability, this potent union of AI and analytics is set to redefine the future of inventory management.

6.1. The Concept of Predictive Analytics in Inventory Management

Predictive analytics is a branch of advanced analytics that uses a plethora of techniques, including data mining, statistical analysis, machine learning, and artificial intelligence, to predict future events based on historical and real-time data. In inventory management, predictive analytics is employed not only to foresee demand and supply patterns but also to optimize stock levels, minimize lead time, and reduce costs.

Predictive analytics enables decision-makers to move away from the traditional reactive approach of inventory management to a more proactive stance. It incorporates various factors like past sales data, current market trends, economic indicators, and seasonal factors to generate accurate demand forecasts. The generated insights facilitate informed decision-making, providing businesses ample time to prepare for anticipated demand or supply changes, thereby ensuring efficiency and reducing waste.

6.2. Advantages of Predictive Analytics in Inventory Management

Predictive analytics ushers in a host of advantages that drastically enhance the efficiency of inventory management.

Accurate Demand Forecasting: By assessing historical sales data, market trends, and various other external variables, predictive analytics can generate accurate demand forecasts. Better forecasting supports optimal inventory levels, reducing the risk of stockouts or overstocks.

Lead Time Reduction: Predictive analytics can analyze past data to identify patterns and anomalies in lead times. This enables businesses to optimize their delivery schedules and reduce overall lead times, enhancing customer satisfaction.

Cost-Efficiency: Excess stock incurs tertiary costs, such as storage, handling, and insurance costs. On the other hand, stock-out situations can result in lost sales and jeopardize customer relationships. Predictive analytics helps maintain optimal inventory levels, thus minimizing such costs and maximizing profits.

6.3. The Application of AI to Predictive Analytics

Artificial Intelligence enhances the ability of predictive analytics by offering in-depth learning abilities, advanced algorithms, and robust computational power. Machine learning, a subset of AI, can handle enormous data sets with diverse variables and identify complex patterns that may be missed by traditional analytics.

Machine learning algorithms enable continuous learning and improvement. Over time, as the AI system is exposed to more data, its forecasts become more accurate, and it's able to make more precise predictions. This dynamic nature of AI makes it a powerful tool in predictive analytics for inventory management.

6.4. Contending with Challenges

While predictive analytics undoubtedly boosts inventory management efficiency, implementing this technology comes with its share of challenges. These can range from issues with data quality, lack of skilled resources, privacy concerns, and technological integration.

Data Quality: Effective predictive analytics heavily relies on high-quality, accurate data. Inconsistent or irregular data can result in inaccurate predictions, negatively influencing business decisions.

Lack of Skilled Resources: Implementing and managing predictive analytics requires skilled resources who can understand and interpret the complex data models. However, there is a scarcity of such professionals, making it challenging for organizations to leverage analytics to its full potential.

Privacy Concerns: Predictive analytics deals with vast amounts of data, some of which may be sensitive. Ensuring data privacy and complying with various regulatory requirements is a significant challenge that businesses have to navigate.

Technological Integration: Predictive analytics must be seamlessly integrated with the current systems for maximum effectiveness. This can be a complex process, demanding substantial resources and time.

Despite these hurdles, the compelling benefits of predictive analytics in inventory management make it worth pursuing.

6.5. Case Studies Illustrating Efficiency Increases

Several organizations have leveraged predictive analytics to propel their inventory management efficiency. For instance, IBM used machine learning to increase visibility into its global supply chain, reducing its inventory costs by $50 million. Cisco, on the other hand, used predictive analytics to improve demand forecasting, reducing stockouts by 30% and lowering inventory holding costs by 65%.

6.6. The Way Forward

As technology continues to advance, predictive analytics is poised to become indispensable to inventory management. The key to successfully implementing predictive analytics lies in understanding the technology's strengths and limitations and investing in the right resources and tools.

Looking ahead, the amalgamation of AI and predictive analytics is set to transform inventory management, making it more responsive, cost-effective, and efficient. For businesses seeking to optimize their supply chain operations, adopting predictive analytics in inventory management is no longer an option but a strategic necessity.

Chapter 7. Unseen Pitfalls: Addressing Challenges in AI Adoption

The rise of AI in logistics and warehouse management promises a future where complex operations are simplified and efficiency is maximized. However, this exciting revolution does not come without its challenges. For organizations looking to integrate AI into their supply chain, understanding these potential pitfalls is just as essential as recognizing the benefits.

7.1. The Challenge of Data Collection, Integration, and Analysis

The concept of successful AI integration in any system revolves around the interplay of data gathering, analysis, and integration. A stumbling block lies in the collection of relevant, high-quality data. Comprehensive warehouse data is necessary for the development of effective machine learning models, and without it, the AI potential remains untapped.

Often, legacy systems may be incapable of generating the required data or may produce data that isn't immediately compatible with AI systems. Even systems that can support data collection often struggle with data fragmentation and a lack of standardization. These inconsistencies can have severe consequences on an AI system's reliability - if erroneous or low-quality data is fed into it, the learning process can be compromised, and it can render incorrect predictions or suggestions.

7.2. Lack of Expertise

While adopting AI solutions is becoming more commonplace, there is a lack of specialized experts in the field. The knowledge gap in understanding and managing AI-driven systems can lead to improper implementation and operation. Many organizations suffer from a dearth of in-house professionals capable of developing or maintaining the AI technology. Contracting third-party services or consultants may bridge this gap, but it could also create dependency and limitations in adapting to specific organizational needs.

In conjunction with this, training employees to interact with AI systems is essential. Without proper training or understanding, the AI's potential can remain largely unexploited, and errors can occur due to incorrect use. This poses an extra effort and financial burden on companies, who must invest in upskilling their workforce.

7.3. Technological Obsolescence and Maintenance

As AI technology evolves at a rapid pace, the risk of technologic obsolescence becomes increasingly relevant. Companies must continually reevaluate and update their systems to incorporate the latest advancements, which requires a significant, ongoing investment of time, effort, and funds. Organizations may face the challenge of integrating these updates into their existing systems without causing disruptions or setbacks.

Just like any other technological system, AI-driven solutions also require regular maintenance and support to resolve faults or failures. However, the complex nature of AI systems can make maintenance tasks more demanding. Troubleshooting and resolving issues with AI technology might require specialist involvement, further raising costs and potentially resulting in downtime.

7.4. Ethical Concerns and Legal Implications

The advent of AI brings up concerns about privacy, worker displacement, and ethics. The data which AI systems rely on might contain sensitive information that, if mishandled, could lead to breaches of privacy. These breaches can have severe legal and reputational implications for your organization.

AI might also alter job roles or replace labor entirely. Though this might enhance efficiency, it raises ethical questions about displacement of workers and societal impacts. While laws are evolving to govern the use of AI, the legal landscape remains uncertain, and organizations must carefully navigate these uncharted territories.

These challenges stress the importance of due diligence, detailed planning, and risk assessment in the AI adoption journey. Yet, it's crucial to remember that these are not reasons to avoid progression. They are merely unseen obstacles lying in the path of AI-driven modernization. By acknowledging potential problems and planning solutions in advance, organizations can pave their way towards efficient, smart warehousing, and logistics.

Chapter 8. Future Forecasts: The Impact of AI on Supply Chain Jobs

Artificial Intelligence (AI) sparked extraordinary changes throughout the supply chain sector. These transformations will undeniably keep accelerating, thus, the future forecast for supply chain jobs in the context of AI is both exciting and complex. The progress in AI and automation has provoked a range of responses, from enthusiasm to scepticism to downright fear about job losses.

8.1. Disruption and Opportunity

There's no denying that AI will disrupt many different jobs within the supply chain sector. In areas where tasks are repetitive and rules-based, we can expect AI to largely replace human labor. For instance, in warehouses, AI-powered robots have begun taking over roles such as packaging items, carrying heavy loads and restocking. At the supply chain planning level, AI can automate processes such as demand forecasting, inventory management, and route optimization.

However, it's important to remember that disruption doesn't necessarily mean elimination. While some jobs may be replaced, many others will be transformed, and entirely new jobs will be created. The evolution of AI creates a demand for professionals who can develop, maintain, and utilize these advanced technologies. Thus, supply chain professionals with skills in AI and machine learning will become highly sought after.

Moreover, the presence of AI can shift the focus of supply chain jobs from transactional tasks to more strategic ones. With AI taking care of the routine operations, humans will have the capacity to concentrate on tasks requiring complex problem-solving, strategic thinking, and interpersonal skills - aspects that are yet to be mastered by AI.

8.2. Reskilling and Upskilling

As AI becomes more ingrained in supply chain processes, there will be a need for workers to reskill or upskill. Reskilling involves learning new skills to perform a different job, while upskilling requires improving abilities or learning advanced skills for the same job role.

For instance, a stock clerk in a warehouse may need to upskill to manage an AI system responsible for inventory management. This shift could also involve reskilling, such as warehouse workers learning to become AI technicians or supply chain data analysts.

This reskilling and upskilling will not be a small task, and it will require significant investment in training and development by organizations. However, it's an investment that promises substantial payoffs in terms of enhanced employee productivity, increased operational efficiency, and competitive advantage.

Education and training institutions will also play a key role in preparing the future workforce for the AI-driven changes. They must revise their curriculum to address the needs of AI-infused supply chain industry, ensuring that students are receiving the relevant and up-to-date training.

8.3. The Augmented Worker

The integration of AI will also lead to the rise of the augmented worker, who is equipped with AI tools to perform their job better and faster. For instance, wearable tech like smart glasses can provide real-time information to warehouse workers to optimize picking routes, and AI voice assistants can help in hands-free order processing.

This means that in many job roles, AI won't necessarily replace humans, but work alongside them to increase efficiency. This collaboration significantly improves decision-making, as combining human intuition with AI's data analysis capabilities can result in more accurate and reliable solutions.

8.4. Agility and Adaptability

In the future, AI will bring an increased level of agility to supply chain jobs. AI-enabled supply chains will be more dynamic and flexible, able to adapt to changing conditions in real-time. This necessitates employees who are comfortable with change, can think on their feet, and continually adapt to new technologies and ways of working.

The use of AI can also enable the supply chain to become more resilient to disruption. By providing real-time insight into supply chain activities and predictive analytics, it can help organizations to anticipate and mitigate risks. As such, professionals skilled in AI and data analytics, who can interpret these insights and make rapid, informed decisions, will be of crucial importance.

In conclusion, the AI revolution promises to be a transformative force across the supply chain sector. While it will inevitably cause disruption, it also brings a multitude of opportunities. By focusing on reskilling/upskilling initiatives and fostering the growth of the augmented worker, supply chain organizations can realize the full potential of AI, ensuring a future that is marked by innovation, efficiency, and strategic decision-making empowered by AI.

Chapter 9. Maximizing Profits: Cost Effectiveness of AI in Logistics

The prospects of Artificial Intelligence (AI) and its forays into logistics cannot be underscored, considering its potential to ramp up efficiency and drive down operational costs. The incorporation of AI into logistics isn't just some far-reaching fantasy; it's a burgeoning reality that has begun to redefine the cost and time-intensive nature of logistics management.

9.1. Revisiting the Traditional Logistics Paradigm

Indeed, the adoption of AI in logistics has been driven by the need to transcend the constraints of traditional frameworks, renowned for their unwieldy and often pecuniary cost. In the conventional order fulfillment process, for instance, everything from inventory management, order consolidation, packing to shipping were primarily done manually which necessitated a significant expenditure in terms of labor.

A brief glance into the workings of traditional warehousing operations will also reveal how inefficiencies creep into the system, sparking an unavoidable spike in costs. A key contributor to these inefficiencies has been the prevalent manually-driven approach towards inventory control. Having employees physically keep track of stock levels, shelf locations, and the tedious process of restocking are all cited as not only time-consuming and error-prone but also a significant drain on resources.

Routinely, companies have also grappled with the inadequacies that come with dynamic demand forecasting. Predicting not only the right quantity but also the right time to stock up on goods has remained somewhat elusive, given the arduous nature of sifting through reams of past sales data manually.

9.2. The Potential of AI in Overhauling Cost Efficiency in Logistics

Mitigating issues like these call for a potent solution, and this is where AI steps in. By harnessing the power of AI, businesses, regardless of size, can optimize their logistics operations, streamline workflows, and effectively drive down costs.

For starters, AI can facilitate smart inventory management by using machine-learning algorithms to track and reorder stock effectively, eliminating human error from the equation. Not only can this lead to improved efficiency, it can have a major impact on cost savings from less overstock and stockouts.

As companies bid adieu to manual data handling, the implementation of AI in demand forecasting stands out as another remarkable stride. AI has the potential to make accurate predictions by neatly analyzing sales histories and external sales determinants (like seasonality, weather, local events etc.). This streamlining of demand forecasting can lead to more optimal inventory levels, saving costs on excess storage and lost sales.

Likewise, AI-powered robotics have proven to be increasingly beneficial, especially in packaging and shipping operations. Automated Guided Vehicles (AGV), which are often armed with AI capabilities, can manage the bulk of material handling tasks, thereby cutting down on labor costs and minimizing damage-related expenses that come with manual handling.

9.3. Quantifying the Cost Benefits of AI in Logistics

If the modern AI-powered logistics is promising a reduction in operational costs, it becomes imperative to quantify these benefits. Many studies across the global logistics landscape have produced compelling statistics that emphasize the economic value of AI.

A case in point is the utilization of AI in inventory management. By streamlining restocking procedures and reducing overstock situations, AI applications have been found to help businesses cut down inventory carrying costs by up to 50%. This is in addition to the cost savings garnered from reducing manual errors and discrepancies.

Advancements in AI-driven demand forecasting have further demonstrated the capacity to curtail costs in the realm of inventory management. With the power to predict demand with higher accuracy, businesses can expect to see a reduction in safety stock requirements by up to 20-50%, implying significant savings.

In terms of labor costs, estimates show that the integration of AI technologies, like automated robotics, can potentially lead to savings of up to 70% in warehouse operations. This is evidenced by the growing number of logistics providers who are tapping into AI to automate their operations.

9.4. The Roadblocks Towards AI Adoption

Despite the evident cost advantages offered by the integration of AI in logistics, there are potential risks and challenges. The initial investment required for AI implementation, resistance from the workforce, and issues with data security and privacy are but a few stumbling blocks.

However, companies must weigh these against the prospective benefits of AI, especially in terms of cost optimization and competitive advantage in the evolving logistics landscape. Precise financial modeling, meticulous risk-versus-reward analysis, and a steadfast commitment to change management from the top downwards would be essential towards successfully navigating these challenges.

9.5. Conclusion: A Vibrant Future Beckons

In an era of unprecedented digital transformation, the marriage of AI and logistics is an exciting herald of change. As these smart systems continue to evolve, they present not only a means to optimize operations but also redefine the conventional notions of cost, time, and resource efficiency. The art of delivering products may fundamentally shift, underpinned by autonomous trucks, predictive analytics, AI-driven drones, and anticipatory logistics. While the journey may be ridden with challenges, the rewards on offer should embolden companies to brave this incipient shift towards smart, AI-driven logistics.

In conclusion, the cost savings presented by AI in logistics are significant but vary from case to case. As a leader in the industry, staying informed about technological progress and carefully studying its potential impact on your specific context will be paramount. This will ensure more effective tactical and strategic decision-making processes, and ultimately, optimal returns on investment.

Chapter 10. Emerging Trends in AI-Driven Logistics and Warehousing

Artificial Intelligence (AI) has started to reshape industries beyond recognition, with logistics and warehousing sitting in the center of this transformative storm. The integration of AI enables innovations that spend the gamut from autonomous mobile robots to digital twins, predictive analytics, and more. With each emerging trend, the landscape of warehousing and logistics further evolves towards a digitally-dominated future.

10.1. The rise of Autonomous Mobile Robots (AMRs)

One of the most visible changes in warehouse operations is the implementation of Autonomous Mobile Robots (AMRs). These AI-driven machines are a step beyond the automated guided vehicles (AGVs) that we've seen in the past. AMRs possess independent navigation abilities, negating the need for a fixed path or guidance infrastructure.

These robots can perform a variety of tasks, from moving inventory to replenishing stocks, with a promise of round-the-clock efficiency. Companies harnessing the power of AMRs have reported substantial boosts in productivity, lowering operational costs, and improved safety.

However, the deployment of AMRs necessitates extensive planning. Considerations need to include the scale of operations, the versatility of tasks, the degree of human-robot collaboration, and the potential disruptions to existing workflows.

10.2. Predictive Analytics to enhance Performance

AI's predictive analytics capabilities are also radically transforming the logistics landscape. Traditional practices relied on static data to make decisions, which resulted in limited foresight and often, reactionary measures. Predictive analytics, on the other hand, leverages machine learning algorithms and real-time data to forecast future events.

This includes anticipating fluctuations in demand, predicting machine maintenance requirements and potential logistical hiccups. This capability allows businesses to be proactive rather than reactive, thereby mitigating risks, streamlining operations, and driving efficiency.

10.3. Digital Twin: A Mirror Image of Physical Assets

The notion of having a 'twin' for each physical asset in a digital space might have seemed far-fetched a few years ago. Today, it's a reality and a rising trend. Digital twins are virtual replicas of physical entities, providing real-time data and insights about their counterparts.

In logistics and warehousing, digital twins unlock an array of applications. They can simulate workflows, assess potential modifications, predict system failures, and evaluate production changes. Although the implementation may be complex and require substantial digitization, the advantages rendered in terms of resource optimization and cost reduction are significant.

10.4. Vision Technology for Quality Management

Another emerging trend in AI-driven logistics and warehousing is the incorporation of vision technology. Combining AI and high-definition cameras pave the way for systems that can identify, categorize, and assess goods automatically.

From inventory management and quality assessment to damage control, the scope of AI-powered vision is limitless. However, the accuracy of such technology is dependent on the quality of data it is trained on. Inaccurate or skewed data can lead to erroneous results.

10.5. AI-Driven Supply Chain Optimization

Staying competitive in today's fast-paced business environment requires not merely meeting customer expectations, but exceeding them. AI-driven supply chain optimization is an emerging trend that facilitates this by enabling precise tracking, improving forecast accuracy, mitigating risks, and identifying bottlenecks before they become problematic.

Through predictive analytics and machine-learning models, AI lends a granular view of the supply chain, allowing for more informed decisions. Yet, streamlining and optimizing a complex supply chain with AI is not a straightforward task. It calls for high data literacy, seamless integrations, and ongoing AI model training.

In conclusion, the realm of AI-driven logistics and warehousing is buzzing with exciting new trends. AMRs are optimizing warehouse operations, predictive analytics is providing invaluable foresight, digital twins are adding a layer of virtual experimentation, vision technology is empowering automatic assessment, and AI-driven supply chain is promising a whole new level of efficiency.

However, the journey towards full AI integration has its challenges. Businesses must surmount the barriers of complexity, data issues, and adaptation to existing structures. Nevertheless, the potential benefits in cost savings, enhanced efficiency, and optimized supply chains offer a future worth striving for.

Chapter 11. Conclusions: Preparing Your Business for the AI Revolution

At this juncture of our study, it is unmistakable that Artificial Intelligence (AI) has inscribed an indelible impression on the warehousing and logistics disciplines. The role it enacted in revolutionizing operations, and the myriad benefits it brings along, attest to its potential as a game-changer. However, the shift towards an AI-driven framework isn't a simple plug-and-play maneuver. Thorough preparation, strategic planning, and an in-depth understanding are intrinsic to any successful AI implementation. As we wrap up this extensive exploration, let's consolidate key insights - assessing the changes to anticipate, strategies to adopt, and some potential points of concern when preparing your business for the AI revolution.

11.1. Embracing the Change

For an enterprise embedded in traditional methods, the integration of AI technologies might seem foreign, even intimidating. Seeking their introduction, then, requires a tangible modification of mentality. Embracing change, when juxtaposed with the premise of the digital transformation, implies a two-fold agenda. On one hand, it's about understanding that the age of digitalization is not an uncertain future but rather an immediate present. On the other hand, it's about a holistic adoption - an acknowledgment that AI's integration will touch every aspect of the business, from operations to customer engagement.

To prepare for this transition, it becomes quintessential to educate oneself and the team about the basics of AI. A comprehension of its functionality, potential applications, and inherent challenges evokes a sense of relatability and diminishes resistance to its adoption. Regular training programs, seminars, workshops, or collaborations with AI providers could serve as fruitful avenues to accumulate this knowledge.

11.2. Structuring and Refining Data Infrastructure

An AI system is as effective as the data it draws upon. Currently, many organizations still struggle with non-standardized data, stored across segregated platforms, in inconsistent formats. This data fragmentation is detrimental to the performance of AI, which thrives on comprehensive, clean, and sorted data. The move towards smart warehousing and logistics, therefore, needs a concurrent refinement of data infrastructure.

To ensure a robust data structure, firms should invest in integrated platforms that allow real-time tracking of data, automate data entry processes to diminish human errors, and implement standardization in data recording. Data privacy policies and security measures should also be put in place in compliance with legal regulations to protect sensitive business and customer information.

11.3. Adapting Operations and Process Flow

AI will invariably demand modifications in business operations and process flows. Automating warehousing and logistics processes may necessitate reviewing and redefining existing Standard Operating Procedures (SOPs). As procedures get automated, certain roles may be repurposed, redefined, or become obsolete. In these instances, it may require the reskilling of the workforce, training them for a business landscape that requires they coexist with AI-centered technologies.

AI integration also introduces changes to inventory management. With predictive analytics in place, AI technology can forecast demand and supply, enabling intelligent inventory planning. This demands businesses to adapt their inventory planning practices, placing trust in the AI's prediction capabilities.

11.4. Formulating an Implementation Strategy

A strategic approach to AI adoption drives the success of its integration. This involves setting clear AI objectives in line with the business goal, defining the scope of AI deployment across operations, and creating necessary budget allocations. It distinguished the activities to be taken up in-house and the ones to be outsourced, identifies key performance indicators to measure the success of AI integration, and charts out a blue-sky strategy considering the overall market trends, competition, and advancements in AI technology.

AI's integration may not fully actualize instantly; it will be a journey. The growth should be envisioned step-by-step, starting small, validating its worth, and then gradually expanding its footprint.

11.5. Preparing for the Challenges

Like all technological advancements, AI carries its set of challenges. It brings along a degree of uncertainty, invites shifts in job roles, exposes vulnerabilities in data security, and may result in inhibitory upfront costs. A segment may also view AI as an intrusive technology, threatening their job security. Mitigating these challenges requires a clear communication strategy that underscores the business's commitment to reskilling and worker safety, a robust cybersecurity framework, and a well-established financial plan that ensures cost-effectiveness in the long run along with the continuous investing in the advancement of the technology.

In conclusion, AI's winds of change have indisputably arrived at the doorstep of warehousing and logistics. The transition has proved auspicious to those who have welcomed it with well-outlined preparations and astute strategic planning. As we stand amidst this transformative phase, it is safe to acknowledge that the AI revolution isn't merely a fleeting trend, but a profound shift shaping the future of the industry. The degree of prosperity, however, lies largely in your hands - in your business's ability to responsively adapt, judiciously strategize, and masterfully execute.